HOW
TO
DE-STRESS

THE ESSENTIAL TOOLKIT
FOR A CALMER LIFE

ANNA BARNES

HOW TO DE-STRESS

Text by Vicki Vrint

An Hachette UK Company
www.hachette.co.uk

Vie Books, an imprint of Summersdale Put
Part of Octopus Publishing Group Limited
Carmelite House
50 Victoria Embankment
LONDON
EC4Y 0DZ
UK

Printed and bound in the Czech Republic

ISBN: 978-1-78685-779-8

Substantial discounts on bulk quantities of Summersdale books are available to corporations, professional associations and other organizations. For details contact general enquiries: telephone: +44 (0) 1243 771107 or email: enquiries@summersdale.com.

Disclaimer
The author and the publisher cannot accept responsibility for any misuse or misunderstanding of any information contained herein, or any loss, damage or injury, be it health, financial or otherwise, suffered by any individual or group acting upon or relying on information contained herein. None of the views or suggestions in this book is intended to replace medical opinion from a doctor who is familiar with your particular circumstances. If you have concerns about your health, please seek professional advice.

CONTENTS

INTRODUCTION   4

Chapter One:
**UNDERSTANDING
STRESS**   6

Chapter Two:
**RELAXATION
TECHNIQUES**   30

Chapter Three:
**A POSITIVE
MENTAL ATTITUDE**   60

Chapter Four:
THE ANTI-STRESS DIET   98

Chapter Five:
**GETTING
PROFESSIONAL HELP**   128

CONCLUSION   159

INTRODUCTION

Most of us feel stressed at some point during our lives and the truth is that it's a natural reaction to the challenges of everyday life. Surprisingly, some stress can even be beneficial to us, by pushing us to get through normal, tricky situations, such as meeting a deadline or passing an exam. But more and more of us are experiencing serious stress on a regular basis, which can stop us from enjoying life and can affect our health, too.

The symptoms of long-term stress can include everything from tiredness and low mood to headaches and disturbed sleep and, with almost 75 per cent of us having felt so stressed we've been overwhelmed or unable to cope (according to a recent study), it's a common problem. Stress can be a contributing factor to many illnesses, so it's important to learn how to control it. The good news is that there are plenty of things you can do to tackle stress (but if you feel that it's becoming too much of a struggle, it's important to talk to your doctor for additional help and advice).

This book includes simple and effective tips to help you combat stress and anxiety. You will learn how to understand your stress triggers, how to de-stress your life and how best to cope in moments when stress does strike.

It's important to take time out to de-stress – even if it's just a short break every day – and you'll find a whole chapter of relaxation tips to guide you with this. There are ideas for speedy de-stressors – ways to help reduce your stress levels in an instant. You'll also learn which foods help you feel calmer and less anxious.

Coping with stress and reducing it are life skills that you can learn, and this book will show you how. Making just a few of these changes will have a positive impact on your stress levels straightaway, and with further work you can make even greater progress and de-stress your life one tip at a time.

CHAPTER ONE

UNDERSTANDING STRESS

Your first step in targeting stress is to learn why it happens. Of course, the reasons we experience stress vary from person to person, but these tips will help you to work out what your personal triggers are, so that you can tackle them one by one. It's also useful to know what happens to you when you go into stress mode. In this chapter, you will discover how to get to grips with your fight-or-flight reflex – your body's response to stress, which is triggered by a release of hormones prompting us to either stay and "fight" the stress or "run away" from it. By understanding it, you can work to dial it down and return to a state of "rest-and-repair" instead, and there are some handy hints on how to do this simply and quickly.

Stress isn't an illness, but it *is* a reaction to our life experiences. Research has found that if we have had a difficult upbringing or experienced a traumatic past we are more likely to suffer from stress — and you may feel that you are more predisposed to this than others. However, studies have shown that the brain is wonderfully adaptive. This chapter shows you how changing your behaviour can affect the way your mind reacts to situations and reduce your anxiety levels. So read on for tips on how to retrain your brain and take control of your stress.

THE GREATEST WEAPON
AGAINST STRESS IS OUR
ABILITY TO CHOOSE ONE
THOUGHT OVER ANOTHER.

WILLIAM JAMES

SPOT
THE
SIGNS

Stress can show itself in a whole range of different ways – from loss of confidence and sleep problems to anger, depression, poor concentration and mood swings. People can experience physical symptoms too, such as dizziness, nausea, sweating, shaking or trembling. Our bodies react in this way in an attempt to deal with mental or physical strain, but we aren't designed to experience them long-term because they can negatively impact our general health. You may even be suffering from stress on an emotional or physical level without realizing it, so take a moment to pause and see if you recognize any symptoms in yourself. If you do, it could be time to take the first steps in tackling your stress.

UNDERSTAND STRESS, ANXIETY AND DEPRESSION

It's useful to understand these terms so that you can work out which may be affecting you.

Stress happens when we feel under pressure in the present moment. It's usually a response to a particular situation, such as moving house or starting a new job.

Anxiety is the worry you feel when you're not specifically "under threat"; it involves concerns about the future or dwelling on the past. The panicky feeling you experience in an exam is stress, but your worrying thoughts about what might happen in the future if you fail are anxiety.

Depression means suffering persistent feelings of low mood that can last weeks or months. Long-term stress can increase the risk of developing depression, if you're not coping with those feelings.

Whether you're stressed, anxious or depressed, taking time for positive action is the most important decision you can make, so you're already on the right track.

KNOW YOUR BODY

Stress can trigger our fight-or-flight response. This reflex is an inheritance from our ancient ancestors: when they perceived a threat in the wild, adrenaline and cortisol were pumped into the bloodstream, increasing the heart rate, breathing and blood pressure, and their muscles tensed to respond to danger. Meanwhile, "non-essential" functions like digestion were slowed down. We still experience this reaction today and sometimes it can be useful – for instance, by helping us deal with critical or dangerous situations. But if you find those symptoms – rapid heartbeat, shallow, rapid breathing and tense muscles – triggered too frequently, by day-to-day events, it can be physically and emotionally draining, and this is when health problems may arise. Learn to sense when your body is entering fight-or-flight mode. Once you recognize the signs, use them as a signal to counteract your fight-or-flight response with some of the methods outlined in this book.

ACTIVATE "REST-AND-REPAIR"

When you understand how your body reacts to stress — by going into fight-or-flight mode — you can use a few easy tricks to feel better in the short term and return to "rest-and-repair" mode (the body's natural, relaxed state). When we're stressed we snatch quick breaths and tense our muscles, so simply stretching and yawning will help us to feel better, or you can try breathing slowly and deeply for a minute to feel an instant sense of calm. People also tend to hold a lot of tension in their jaw (perhaps gritting their teeth), or in their neck (hunching the shoulders), so take a moment to consciously relax these muscles and you'll feel better for it. Make a point of trying these quick fixes regularly throughout the day — whenever you check your phone or make a drink, for example — and you'll be taking your first steps to actively de-stress.

THE FIRST STEP IN MOVING FORWARD

IS DECIDING THAT YOU'RE NOT GOING TO STAY WHERE YOU ARE

TAKE NOTE OF YOUR STRESS

//

One of the best things you can do to tackle stress is to identify the specific events or situations that cause it, and you can do this by keeping a physical record of your stress. Over the course of a fortnight, make a note of any moments when you feel stressed or concerned, including minor "blips" as well as more obvious events. Write down when and where they occurred, what you were thinking or doing at the time, and give your stress level a rating from one to ten. After two weeks, you should have a good idea of where and when your most stressful moments occur. Make a list of these stress triggers (see next tip) and keep it close to hand as time goes on. It could prove to be a great tool for working through your worries and planning some positive steps forward.

TARGET YOUR TRIGGERS

Look through your list of stress triggers one at a time and see how many you can eliminate from your week. If you can't avoid them completely perhaps you can de-stress them to some extent. A common trigger for many people is the daily commute to work: could you improve yours by taking a different route? Or could you walk, car share, change your hours or work from home more regularly? If your job itself is the problem, can you talk to your boss and improve your situation? Or is it even time you applied for something new? Be as creative with your solutions as possible and write your ideas down. Don't be afraid to discuss them with your friends; they might come up with a solution that hasn't crossed your mind.

DE-STRESS YOUR SCHEDULE

One of the most common causes of stress is the sheer number of commitments many of us face on a day-to-day basis. It's not unusual for people to spend their whole day rushing from one thing to the next without a break. Under this sort of pressure we don't have time to relax or recuperate, and we may not be able to carry out our responsibilities properly, which can lead to feelings of guilt and further stress. Cut down on your obligations and delegate or share them where possible. Be realistic about what you agree to do and learn to say no, without feeling guilty. Bear in mind that it's quality rather than quantity that counts, and that by reducing the number of tasks or engagements you take on, you're increasing the amount of time you can spend on the things that are really important to you.

A DE-STRESS PLAN

If you don't have any obvious causes of stress in your life but feel anxious or on edge a lot of the time, it may seem that there's nothing you can do to improve things. Don't despair. (Once you start to feel stressed, you tend to be more sensitive to further stress – creating a cycle – so it's much more important to learn how to control your anxious feelings than to pin down the cause.) Prepare some calming, stress-busting tips for tricky moments and keep a list of these in your pocket or on your phone. Your list could include ideas such as: carry out a mindfulness exercise; phone a friend; go for a quick walk; listen to your favourite music track. That way you'll be prepared if stress strikes out of the blue.

GET ACTIVE

When we exercise, our bodies produce "happy hormone" serotonin and reduce "stress hormone" cortisol, which is why regular exercise can improve your mood. Exercise is also a great way of releasing tension – your worries tend to fade away when you're pushing yourself to complete that extra mile! Many exercises have the added advantage of getting you out and about, which will also boost your mood. There are plenty of different ways you can include exercise in your daily routine, including free options such as jogging and walking, or trying an online tutorial in yoga or dancing, for example. Exercise is good for your self-confidence, too; it's satisfying to see your stamina improve with regular training. Why not set yourself a fitness target to keep motivated? There are lots of phone apps that are ideal for this, as they outline regular exercise routines to help you reach your goal.

GO WITH THE FLOW

It's often the case that our worries are based on events that are out of our control. We can feel frustrated when things don't go to plan, or become anxious about the future, pinning our hopes on a particular outcome. However, it's important to be realistic about what we can and can't control in life. Next time you start to feel stressed, remind yourself that you can't always be in charge of events around you but you can learn to control your emotions and the way you deal with them. Start each day with the thought, "I will cope with whatever today brings". Try not to spend your time pondering the "what ifs" that may or may not come true – research has found that 85 per cent of our worries never actually happen anyway! Also, bear in mind that even if your worst fears do become reality, you'll deal with them in the best way you can and seek support if necessary.

FIGHT PANIC

A panic attack is an intense fight-or-flight response: symptoms include breathlessness, sweating and increased heart rate. Although a panic attack can feel all-consuming and very frightening at the time, it isn't dangerous, won't cause you physical harm and will always pass. If you suffer from panic attacks, it helps to have a plan in place to deal with them. When you first notice the signs, recognize what's happening and remind yourself that you'll be fine. Sit down if you can, close your eyes and focus on your breathing. Breathe in slowly for four seconds, hold your breath for two seconds and breathe out for six seconds. As you steady your breathing, try to relax your muscles too. It might help to focus on an object nearby and study it mindfully, noting all the details, as this can help you tune out distractions. When you feel able, have a low-sugar snack, such as a piece of fruit (citrus fruits in particular have been found to reduce anxiety because of the boost in vitamin C they provide), and sip some water to help you recover.

AVOID SECOND-HAND STRESS

If it's the people you meet, rather than the situations you encounter, that add to your stress levels, try to limit contact with anxiety-inducing colleagues, friends or family. It's possible to pick up on other people's stress – something which can happen very easily at work – so avoid any negative chatter in the workplace if you can. If you find yourself chatting to a serial complainer, try to steer the conversation down a more positive route or, if all else fails, make your excuses and leave, rather than absorbing their negativity. You may find that a friend's stress levels are affecting you if they constantly use you as a sounding board for their problems or take their frustrations out on you. While it's important and noble to support others, you shouldn't find yourself doing this to the detriment of your own well-being. Being honest with your friend about the situation is key – and if they aren't willing to change the dynamic in your relationship, it might be time to take a gentle step back for your own good.

ASSUME NOTHING!

//

Many of our stressful thoughts are based on false assumptions — when we wrongly assume something to be true. These unfounded ideas can have a damaging effect on our state of mind, from fearing that past experiences will repeat themselves to making pessimistic projections of what the future might hold. Perhaps you're worrying that you've done something to offend a friend who blanked you when you walked past them in the street? Or you think your boss isn't happy with something you've submitted because you haven't yet had a positive response? These scenarios all involve assumptions, and next time you make one, stop your thoughts in their tracks and ask yourself whether there is a more likely explanation. Perhaps your friend didn't notice you because they had something on their mind, or your boss hasn't had time to read your report yet? Learn to stick to the facts rather than following your negative assumptions — or you could end up wasting time by worrying over nothing.

ENJOY ALPHA WAVES

When we're stressed, the electrical impulses in our brains – known as brain waves – go into overdrive, which is why it can be so hard for us to turn off our racing thoughts. When we're relaxed and not processing too much information, however, our brain goes into "alpha wave" mode: a zen-like state that helps us to feel calm and safe. You can learn to dial down your brain activity and induce alpha waves – which fall in the middle of the brain wave spectrum – through meditation, breathing exercises and yoga. Another method is to listen to stress-reducing tunes that will trigger alpha wave activity – look online for free recordings of this type of music. You could even make your own stress-relieving sounds by trying an easy drumming technique.

REBRAND YOURSELF!

Our brains are amazingly adaptive and we can use that to our advantage when combatting stress. Studies have shown that taking part in activities such as meditation, volunteering or practising positivity can actually change the physical make-up of your brain, boost your mood and make you more inclined to behave optimistically in the future. So if you've started to think of yourself as an anxious person or a bit of a pessimist the good news is that you can train your brain to react more positively. Try writing a list of five positive characteristics you would like to embody moving forward, such as: optimism, understanding, enthusiasm, self-possession, sincerity – and carry this list with you. Make a conscious effort to exhibit these qualities whenever you can, because "faking it until you make it" really can work.

SET YOUR GOALS

As you start to understand your stress triggers and surrounding emotions a little more, it's a good idea to set yourself some stress-busting goals, so that you have something practical to work on. These don't need to be too specific. You may simply want to learn how to relax more, deal with work related stress or improve your quality of sleep. Make a heading for each goal in your stress diary and jot down some ideas for trying to achieve them, using tips in this book to help. For example, you might decide to try meditating every evening, attend a course on stress-management, or reorganize your bedroom and invest in some new bedding. Keep a record of your de-stressing attempts and how effective they are.

CHAPTER TWO

RELAXATION

TECHNIQUES

Relaxation is the number one skill you can learn to help you combat stress. There is a mass of evidence that shows the link between using relaxation techniques and reducing stress levels. The problem with our increasingly busy lifestyles is that it can seem difficult to fit precious downtime into our day.

The importance of making time for physical exercise is well known and widely recognized. However, taking care of our mental well-being — with meditation or mindfulness exercises, or even just ten minutes of quiet time each day — is equally vital. If we don't look after our emotional health, the chances are that our physical well-being will suffer in the long-run too.

This chapter includes tips on how to fit relaxation into your day, no matter how busy you are, and shows you how doing the things you love can have a huge impact on reducing your stress levels. There are tips covering meditation, improving your sleep quality, relaxing treatments you can try and even apps you can use to aid relaxation. Don't underestimate the importance of "me time", and be sure to make relaxation a part of your day.

TAKE REST; A FIELD
THAT HAS RESTED GIVES
A BOUNTIFUL CROP.

OVID

MAKE TIME TO RELAX

Many of us feel guilty if we take some time out for ourselves, and even if we set some time aside we end up filling it with odd chores. In fact, we often afford more care and attention to our cars or phones than we do to looking after our own mental well-being! Schedule in some regular relaxation time every day. Before you get up in the morning, think about your day and when you'll be able to fit in some time to yourself. Could you spend 15 minutes walking outside during your lunch break? How about going up to bed a little earlier and meditating before you sleep? Add a regular "date with yourself" to your calendar too. When you do have that precious time to yourself, make sure you give 100 per cent of your attention to whatever relaxing activity you pick – whether it's catching up on your favourite drama or spending half an hour on your latest hobby.

FIND
YOUSELF
A HAVEN

It's important to have a calm and quiet place where you can take time out, particularly if you'd like to try a relaxation method such as meditation. Give some thought to the best place for your haven and make it as comfortable and pleasant as possible. Even if you don't have a room to yourself, try to find a favourite corner – perhaps with a comfortable chair – where you won't be disturbed. Invest in some cosy cushions or a throw, and find a little storage space for your relaxation tools, whether it's your favourite book, your journal, craft supplies or a music speaker. If you have room to put up an inspirational picture or two, that's even better. Visit your "retreat" at least once a day, if you can, to really feel the benefits.

FOCUS ON YOUR BREATHING

//

The simplest and quickest way to relax is to concentrate on your breathing. Although breathing is, of course, a natural process, spending a few minutes each day focusing on breathing can help to reduce your stress levels and lower your blood pressure. Breathing deeply sends a message to your brain to calm down, which then translates to your body. So aim to breathe in deeply and slowly through the nose to a count of four so that your abdomen rises; then exhale steadily through the mouth. If it helps, you can rest a hand on your belly to make sure you're breathing into the right place. As you breathe out, feel your stress and tension leave your body. If you want to try more advanced breathing techniques, such as methods related to yoga practice, check online for different examples.

CULTIVATE MINDFULNESS

To do something mindfully means to focus on experiencing it fully, in the moment. Mindfulness is a wonderful antidote to stress as it prevents our minds from dwelling on things that have happened in the past or worrying about what might happen in the future. You can do anything mindfully – simply focusing on your breathing (see page 36) is an exercise in mindfulness. Other easy mindful tasks to try include going to the window and focusing on the colours, patterns and textures you see; listening to a new piece of music and immersing yourself in the sound; or doing an everyday task in a mindful way, such as getting dressed while taking in the details of the clothing you are wearing. Concentrating on the present moment is very calming as you're reminding yourself that all is currently well, and you have no need to worry.

MAKE TIME FOR MEDITATION

Meditating is a great de-stressing tool. With a little practice, you can learn to disengage from your worries and calm your mind wherever you are. There are hundreds of apps, podcasts and classes available to teach you how to meditate, but you can try it at home very easily. Sit comfortably: don't worry too much about where and how, just relax and release any tension in your muscles. Focus on something repetitive, such as your breathing, or you could try visualising a sequence of colours or chanting a mantra. Put simply, a mantra is a word or sound repeated to aid concentration in meditation. It's up to you what you chant, of course, but the most widely known mantra – used in many religions including Hinduism and Buddhism – is "Om" (pronounced "Aum"). Don't feel frustrated if other thoughts intrude unexpectedly during your meditation. Distracting thoughts can be part of the process and it doesn't mean that you're doing anything wrong; just gently bring your mind back to your focal point – your breathing, visualisations or mantra. Practise daily if possible, just for a couple of minutes at first, and you should find it easier to relax and calm your mind as time goes on. If you feel you need extra help, try guided meditation tutorials.

GUIDED MEDITATION

//

Guided meditations involve a narrator or teacher taking your imagination on a journey where you visualize yourself in a dreamlike setting. They can be very absorbing and relaxing and are the perfect introduction to meditation as your attention is gently drawn away from your day-to-day worries. You can find hundreds of pre-recorded guided meditations online – many for specific purposes, such as tackling stress or sleep problems. You could even record your own meditations or try your own visualizations by imagining yourself walking through a beautiful wood or along a beach, for example. It can help to picture yourself walking down a series of steps or along a path as you enter your visualization, so that you can imagine yourself feeling more and more relaxed as you progress. Don't be in too much of a hurry to return to the real world at the end of your meditation – give yourself time to "wake up" slowly.

TEACH YOURSELF PMR

Progressive Muscle Relaxation — or PMR — is easy to learn, and a very effective way of relaxing the body and releasing stress. The technique involves mindfully tensing and then releasing each of the muscle groups in your body in turn, working from your head to your feet. By focusing on tensing your muscles before relaxing them, you are able to relax them more fully and, with practice, you can learn to relax your whole body very quickly. Starting with your face, lightly clench your muscles as you breathe in and then relax them as you breathe out. Work down through your neck, shoulders, arms and upper body, to your torso, lower body and legs, taking each limb in turn and finishing with your feet. This is a good exercise to practise in bed before you drift off to sleep.

PRACTISE
YOGA

_____

With its gentle movements and focus on holding specific poses, yoga is the ideal antidote to stress. Yoga helps you to disengage from stressful thoughts and worries as it brings your awareness to your body and is very grounding. The relaxing effects of this ancient Indian practice are well documented, and many sessions finish with a short meditative cool down session where you consciously relax your body one part at a time (see page 41). Yoga also includes breathing exercises, which help you achieve a deeper state of relaxation, and these can be practised anywhere. Look for a beginners' course near you, or try an online tutorial at home to get you started.

TAKE
A DIP

To unwind after a stressful day, nothing beats a relaxing bath, so pick (at least) one evening a week to enjoy a really indulgent, unhurried soak. Make sure you have all the essential ingredients to hand – clean fluffy towels, candles, music and a good book are all great options. You could treat yourself to your favourite bath bubbles or go for a more natural approach – a salt bath can work wonders if you're detoxing (mentally or physically). Add around a kilo of rock salt (Himalayan rock salt is a great choice) to your bath water, which should be as close to body temperature as possible. The salt draws toxins out of the body, and is also a good source of minerals, which can be absorbed through the skin. Don't forget to rehydrate with a glass of water after your soak.

A GOOD NIGHT'S SLEEP

Getting a good night's sleep can be a challenge when we're feeling anxious, and poor sleep – and the resulting tiredness – can make us feel even more stressed the next day. Improve your chances of drifting off to sleep by making your bedroom free from distracting clutter and technology. Think about soft lighting, and ensure that the room temperature is not too warm or cold. Instil a relaxing bedtime routine – a warm bath, a non-caffeinated drink and some quiet time before sleep. You can use this time to reflect back on the day, write in your journal or meditate. If this is the first opportunity you've had to relax since getting up, you may find all the day's worries foremost in your mind. Try to offload these before bed – you could even schedule in some "worry time" at this point in the evening to clear your head.

GET INTO THE ZONE

Pick an activity that you're really good at and do it regularly! Playing to your strengths will remind you of your abilities and improve your self-confidence: when you do something that you're naturally good at you'll be doing it effortlessly. You'll have that wonderful feeling of being in the zone – and studies have shown that your brain is in a naturally more relaxed state when you're occupied in this way. So whether it's excelling at your favourite sport, acing a pub quiz, playing an instrument or even writing a poem, work out what your feel-good activity is and make time for it at least once a week. It could be your best de-stressor.

WRITE IN A JOURNAL

Keeping a journal can help you to unwind at the end of the day. It's also something good to focus on if you've decided to set aside ten minutes of quiet time with all devices and screens turned off (see page 94) before bed. Your journal can be used for anything you fancy – whether it's keeping a track of your stress levels and triggers (page 17) or just as an outlet for your thoughts. If you're feeling creative, bullet journaling is a brilliant way of putting your artistic skills to use and staying organized too. There are many inspirational ideas for this online, but you can design pages for everything from tracking your mood and your progress with adopting positive habits, to more structured financial records or lists of your goals and weekly tasks. How about including a "one-line-a-day" page, where you write just one thought or memory each day, to read back at the end of the month?

HAVE A MASSAGE

Massage is a great stress-reliever. The massage itself will relax your muscles, soothe aches and pains and encourage healthy blood flow throughout your body. It's also very relaxing to take time out from the hectic pace of your day, with aromatherapy oils and soothing music adding to the calming experience. It should be easy to find the details of massage therapists near you; different types of massage are available (such as hot stone massage, sports massage or shiatsu) depending on your specific needs.

Note: If you're using essential oils, remember that these natural substances can have powerful effects, so it's wise to test a small amount on your skin to check for any reaction. Always consult a physician before use, particularly if you are pregnant, nursing or have a known health issue.

TOUCH THE BODY, HEAL THE MIND,

CALM THE SPIRIT

DE-STRESS YOUR HOME

It's hard to relax when we're surrounded by clutter, and it's even harder to be organized. If you constantly find yourself rushing around looking for essential items, you're needlessly adding to your stress levels. Decluttering your home may not seem like the most appealing task but the benefits are too good to ignore. Not only will you feel calmer and more relaxed if you're living in a well-organized space, but you'll save time on cleaning, tidying and searching for things too. Although it can be hard to get started, you may find the act of decluttering surprisingly cathartic. Tackle the area that causes you the most stress first. Be ready for action by labelling three bags or boxes – one to keep (for items you can't part with or still need), one to donate (for unwanted but usable items that can be given to charity or to friends or family) and one to throw away (if the item is broken or unusable). Once every item has been placed in one of these containers, distribute or dispose of them accordingly – and make sure that every item you're keeping has a suitable place to live in your home. Decluttering in 15-minute bursts can be very effective and less intimidating so set a timer and have a quick blitz – you'll feel much better for it.

GROUND YOURSELF

//

Stress may leave us feeling panicky, but "grounding" can counteract this. There are different methods you can try and anything that involves contact with nature is effective. Lying on the grass may sound crazy, but it is actually very calming to relax on the ground, gazing up at the clouds or trees. Alternatively, either sit at the foot of a tree or imagine that you are doing so, and visualize calming energy flowing into your body from the ground beneath you. When stress strikes, breathe deeply and revisit this image and the feeling of calm connectedness. Some people carry a crystal or smooth stone in their pocket to use for grounding – just relax, focus on your breathing and hold your chosen object in your palm, picturing calming earth energy flowing from it and into you. If you have no props to hand, plant your feet firmly on the ground and picture the grounding energy flowing into your body that way instead.

USE ACUPRESSURE

Acupressure is a therapy originating in ancient China which clears blockages in the body's *qi* (chi) - a Chinese word which means "life energy". It works by applying pressure to specific points on the body. You can visit an acupressure therapist for treatment, but there are easy ways you can relieve your own stress with acupressure. For an instant feeling of calm, massage the webbing between your index finger and thumb using the index finger and thumb of your opposite hand. Another easy acupressure point is three finger widths below your wrist crease, in between the "tramline" tendons of your arm. Massage both your left and right arm with the opposite index finger for stress relief (and also to ease motion sickness). Try to breathe slowly and deeply into your belly as you carry out your DIY acupressure exercises.

HAPPY APPS

There are plenty of apps around that can help you to relax and tackle stress, so search online for some reviews of the different options to see what appeals to you most. Apps like Headspace and Calm are a great place to start: they teach you to meditate and tackle stress at the same time, while other apps (such as SAM and Happify) use psychological theory to help you boost your mood or manage stress symptoms. You can even indulge in some mindful mandala (circular symbols representing the universe in Hinduism and Buddhism) virtual colouring on your phone while you're on the bus or sign up to receive a "good deed for the day" challenge and feel the mood-boosting benefits of helping others.

FIND SLOW MOMENTS

If your day is a mad rush of things to do and you regularly find your stress levels rising, pick one daily task to be your slow-down trigger. How about making your bed slowly and deliberately each morning, smoothing down the sheets and positioning the pillows before you move on to the rest of the day? Or you could turn your afternoon cup of tea into a relaxing routine – take a few minutes to set a tray with a milk jug and teapot and sit down and savour your drink, as you take stock of your day. This will force you to stop dashing about and switch down a gear on a daily basis, and can have a big impact on your stress levels across the week.

TRY ESSENTIAL OILS

Essential oils, which are plant extracts, have natural stress-relieving qualities. They can be inhaled or used in massage (many need to be mixed in a carrier oil if they are being used on the skin). When essential oils are inhaled, the scent triggers a calming reaction in other areas of our brain, lowering our heart rate, blood pressure and stress levels. When used on the skin, they soothe the muscle tension caused by stress (and still smell good too, of course). Vanilla, lavender, rose and jasmine are all popular for countering stress. You can add a few drops to your bath, or sprinkle some onto a tissue to breathe in during the day or onto your pillow at night. Alternatively use a diffuser to spread their relaxing effects throughout your home.

Note: As mentioned on page 49, it's important to take care when using essential oils. These natural substances can have powerful effects, so it's wise to test a small amount on your skin to check for any reaction. Always consult a physician before use, particularly if you're pregnant, nursing or have a known health complaint.

FREE WRITING

Free writing is often used as a practice exercise by authors wanting to encourage their creativity. However, it has benefits for everyone and is an interesting way to relax and de-stress. Put simply, it involves writing continuously for a set length of time without worrying about style or content. All you need is a pen and paper, or a laptop if you'd rather type, and some time to sit quietly and free your thoughts. Choose a time limit – five minutes is a good starting point – and then put your pen to paper, or fingers to the keys, and begin. Don't ponder too long over your subject matter, or pause to consider spelling and grammar, the idea is to write whatever comes into your head and keep going. The repetitive act of writing is soothing in itself and, if you give your mind free rein, you may get a sneaky peek at your unconscious thoughts when you read your words back at the end of your session.

CHAPTER THREE

A POSITIVE MENTAL ATTITUDE

When you're suffering from stress it can be very easy to get stuck in a pattern of negative thinking. Stress can even make us turn down opportunities to do the very things that could help us to de-stress, because we feel overwrought or anxious. But don't despair; we can change the way we behave and break the hold stress has over us by developing a positive mental attitude. Even small changes can make a difference and by consciously thinking and acting in a more positive manner, we can even change the way our brain works and develop a calm, optimistic approach to counteract our stress.

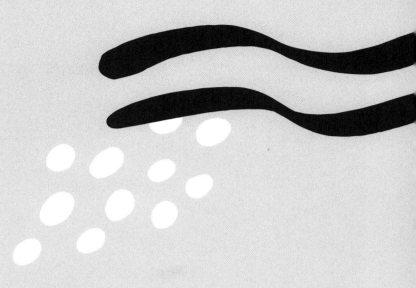

You can learn to develop a positive mental attitude in almost every situation – whether you're stuck in a queue or facing up to a challenging event – and this chapter will show you how to do it. There are also plenty of tips on how to stop your negative thoughts in their tracks and replace them with positive affirmations, to give you the confidence to tackle whatever the day might bring.

Cultivating a can-do attitude will benefit you in every area of your life. You'll certainly feel cheerier and less stressed, but you're also more likely to enjoy better relationships and go on to achieve more in other areas too, so read on and embrace the power of positivity.

IF YOU CHANGE THE WAY
YOU LOOK AT THINGS,
THE THINGS YOU LOOK
AT CHANGE.

WAYNE DYER

SAP YOUR NEGATIVE THINKING

How often do you find yourself believing your own negative self-talk? Our internal chatter can involve a whole raft of negative thoughts – "I'll never be ready to take my driving test" or "Why didn't I cycle to work like that guy... I'm so unfit" – which can trigger anxious feelings. These can hold us back from achieving our full potential, so next time you find yourself thinking along these lines try the following:

- **Stop** your negative thought in its tracks
- **Acknowledge** that it's unhelpful, and replace the thought with a
- **Positive** affirmation such as "I can do this – I'm strong and calm"

If you do this regularly you'll find yourself starting to take a more positive approach to life and your abilities. You'll feel more confident when you see the great results you achieve too.

PICK POSITIVE AFFIRMATIONS

Positive affirmations aren't just powerful tools for derailing your negative self-talk; you can also use powerful positive statements to help you calm down in those moments when you go into fight-or-flight mode. A good mantra to remember when stress strikes is: "All is well – I am safe". Focusing on this reminds you that you're not facing any physical threat and have no need to panic. If you look back at your list of stress triggers (see page 17) you may be able to think of more specific affirmations to help you cope with your stressful scenarios. If you get anxious presenting at work meetings, you could use "If I put my mind to it, I can achieve it", or try repeating "I can't control the traffic but I can control my mood" during delays on your commute!

BREAK DOWN TRICKY TASKS

//

In times of stress, even the most basic tasks can seem overwhelming, and we can end up putting things off, making our stress levels worse. Breaking tasks down into manageable chunks makes them much less intimidating. If you need to fill in a form, for example, start by gathering the materials you need. Then, once you're ready, tackle the easiest section first and go on to complete one question at a time, whenever you feel able to. If your task is more complicated, write down the steps you need to take and work through them gradually. (Generally, if you start to feel panicked, focusing on finishing whatever you are doing *right now* – walking into work or completing a phone call – is a good way of regaining control.) Believe that if you set your mind to something, you can do it – if you take it one step at a time.

THREE
A DAY

Most of us are familiar with the concept of eating "five a day" when it comes to looking after our diet, but many of us don't think about doing something every day to boost our emotional well-being. It's important to make an effort to do things that are beneficial to your mental health, so embrace the concept of "three a day" and see if you can fit in three stress-reducing activities before bedtime. You could start the day by listening to your favourite song before you get out of bed, read a book for 15 minutes in your lunch break and end the day with a relaxing bath... or why not meet up with a friend in the evening, take a walk to the park together and laugh on the way to score three de-stress points in one go?

FINE-TUNE YOUR FINANCES

Money issues are a common cause of stress and it can be all too easy to adopt a head-in-the-sand approach to them, but you will feel better if you take positive and practical steps towards financial responsibility. Start by taking stock of your financial situation and working out your incomings and outgoings, then create a suitable monthly budget – using a financial app could be helpful for this. Streamline your outgoings by cancelling subscriptions and buying non-branded groceries and clothes, checking out the best deals for energy and insurance, and paying off debts before you save. If your money problems are spiralling out of control, don't be afraid to ask for help. There is plenty of free support out there, from money-management courses to debt counselling, so that you can work on leaving your money worries behind.

FOCUS ON HOW BLESSED YOU ARE, NOT HOW STRESSED YOU ARE

CELEBRATE YOUR STRENGTHS

When we get caught up in a cycle of stress, our self-confidence can plummet and we may even start to judge ourselves harshly for feeling stressed, which in turn makes us feel even lower. To break this negative cycle, focus on your strengths. Make a list of your achievements – the things that you're really proud of – and note the qualities you have that made these possible. You could put together a mood board or page in your journal to celebrate your strengths. If you're feeling stuck, ask a friend what they admire about you – you could exchange compliments and start by telling them why **you** value **them** as a friend. Why not include a section for this sort of positivity in your journal: you could collect compliments or positive achievements, and end the day by focusing on these rather than those needlessly negative thoughts.

DON'T BOTTLE IT UP

It's important to let negative emotions out, so that we can go on to take a positive approach to life's challenges. Stress can build up when we suppress emotions, and whether it's frustration, anger, guilt or sorrow, our bodies are not designed to store these feelings up. Strong emotions cause us to produce stress hormones, and the most effective way of releasing them is through crying. It's our body's natural stress-release mechanism, and you shouldn't suppress the urge to do it when you're upset. Studies have shown that tears contain stress hormones, and some research reveals a high incidence of stress-related conditions, such as stomach ulcers, in patients who don't release their emotions through crying. If you're feeling angry or upset, taking a moment to cry it out will leave you feeling calmer and clear the decks ready for you to take a positive approach once you've let those feelings go.

EXHALE AS YOU EXERCISE

Exercises that encourage you to focus on your breathing are very effective de-stressors and will leave you feeling brighter and ready for the day's challenges. Swimming is a good example. With its regular repetitive movements and breathing pattern, it encourages you to focus on the mechanics of your body, rather than your worries. Tai chi is also an excellent option, with another benefit being that classes often take place outside. This ancient Chinese martial art is called "moving meditation" because those who practise it focus on the flow of precise and gentle movements, feeling calm and in control as a result. Alternatively, you could try Pilates, another relaxing practice that not only improves flexibility but encourages you to be present.

CHALLENGE UNHELPFUL THOUGHTS

Try challenging specific worries to see just how realistic they are. Start by writing your worry down: "I'm worried that I'll make a fool of myself on my training course", for example. Now ask yourself the following:

1. What evidence is there to back up your worry?
2. How will you feel about this in a year's time?
3. What are the pros and cons of thinking this way?
4. How can you reframe this situation in a positive light?
5. What would you say to a friend who was feeling this way?

In this example, you have no evidence to base your worry on; you probably won't remember the worry over the course in a year's time; there's no benefit to your worry, but the downside is that it's making you stressed; you can see the course as a welcome break from work, and you'd tell a friend that they'd be fine.

STAY CALM
IN A QUEUE

Unavoidable delays always seem to happen when we're in a rush to get somewhere and the frustration of being stuck can ramp up our stress levels in seconds. No amount of getting worked up will make these hitches pass any quicker, though, so the best thing to do is to have a plan prepared for these moments. If you can learn to stay calm while queuing, you can learn to stay calm in other stressful moments when events are beyond your control. Good ways to beat queue stress include: listening to a podcast, singing along to your favourite track, guessing the next rhyming lyric in a song, or practising your breathing (page 36) or progressive muscle relaxation exercises (page 41). If all else fails try to see the bright side – you have a bonus half an hour to yourself, without interruptions!

BLOW OFF SOME STEAM!

//

When the frustrations of everyday life build up, the trick is to release them in an appropriate way and, thankfully, there are many activities that can help you do this. For day-to-day stress release, exercise is a great option (see page 21), whether it's a dance class or playing your favourite sport. Many people find that losing themselves in something creative is very effective too. Singing along to a favourite song can be cathartic, or for releasing more deep-rooted stress tremoring therapy can have great results (see page 113). And if you can think of an activity that combines the stress-busting effects of touch, intimacy, exercise and deep breathing – well, that's got to be a good option too.

MOVING ON

Many anxious thoughts are the results of negative experiences we've had in the past. We may find ourselves worrying unduly that the experience might happen again, or perhaps we're re-living awkward encounters that happened weeks ago. These thoughts are not only stressful (and, as a result, bad for our well-being), but fruitless too, because we can't change the past. Don't let the past spoil your present – you can learn from it and move on instead. Take a look through your list of worries and think about those that have their roots in the past. Make a conscious move to leave these past imposters behind by writing down a summary of what happened and how it made you feel. Read through this and think of the lesson(s) you can learn from it – note them in your journal, if you like. Then it's probably best to bin, bury or burn your account of the past. It has served its purpose and you're ready to move on into positivity.

PHONE POSITIVITY

Many of us spend way too much time online, and often the things that we're looking at can make our stress levels worse. Perhaps we're checking work emails, browsing gloomy news stories or experiencing a social-media-induced inferiority complex when we should be relaxing. Use your phone to boost your mood instead by putting together a file of your cheeriest photos from trips out, creating a playlist of your favourite upbeat tunes or subscribing to posts that spread positivity or help you relax. You could even record a mood-boosting message on your voice recorder app to cheer you up when you're feeling low – or get a friend, loved one or pet to record one for you!

DON'T PUT IT OFF!

Whether it's sending a tricky email or organizing a dental check-up, you're not doing yourself any favours if you put off the tasks you dread. You're going to have to do these things eventually and it's much less stressful to bite the bullet and get on with them, instead of brooding over them and adding to your anxiety levels. Pick a task that's been worrying you for a while and get it done today – you'll feel so much better for it. It's not just the items on our to-do lists that can end up preying on our minds, we can also procrastinate over decisions far longer than is needed. If you've been pondering a dilemma for too long, take action. Trust your gut instinct and move forward with courage or, if you're really stuck, get some additional advice. Where possible, deal with problems immediately rather than giving them a chance to weigh on your mind.

PET
AN
ANIMAL

There is no denying that spending time with animals is good for our well-being – studies have even found that it can reduce our stress levels. Stroking a pet is a mindful activity in itself as it forces us to be still and concentrate on our furry (or scaly, or feathery) friend. When you add in the affection that a pet can offer back in return, it's easy to understand how contact with animals is such a mood-booster. Pets also set us a good example when it comes to beating stress. They live in the moment, they can't be rushed and they put their own needs first, making sure they get plenty of rest. We can't all disappear for a catnap halfway through a shift at work, but we can learn to take time out when we need it. If you don't have an animal of your own, you could spend time with a friend's pet or visit or volunteer (see page 86) at a local animal shelter.

PICK
POSITIVE
PEOPLE

The people we spend time with have a huge impact on our mood and well-being, so try to avoid anyone who elevates your stress levels (see page 24) and pick positive companions when you can. Spending time with your friends and family is one of the best ways to de-stress. What could be better than feeling relaxed, being yourself and laughing while feeling loved and appreciated at the same time? Be sure to make time for positive interactions as often as possible. If you can't meet up with your precious people every day, have regular calls or chats online – and don't spend the whole time going over your latest worries. Of course it's good to get advice from a valued friend, but ensure that the conversation goes both ways and share a cheery anecdote or two, or relive a favourite memory, to include a positive vibe. Planning things to look forward to with friends is also a good mood-booster.

BE A VOLUNTEER

Volunteering has plenty of benefits for stress-sufferers (and, indeed, anyone who gives it a try). Spending time with others is beneficial in itself, but giving something back to a worthwhile cause is also very rewarding. Volunteers get a great sense of purpose from their activities: knowing that other people are depending on you will increase your self-esteem and self-confidence. It can also help you to focus on something other than your own worries, as you may well be working with people who are experiencing challenging situations. It can really give you a different perspective on your own life situation. In short, doing good does you good. Check online for volunteering opportunities near you.

BE A WARRIOR, NOT A WORRIER

TRY SOMETHING NEW

For stress-sufferers, it's very easy to feel that our lives are stuck in a rut and it can be especially hard to break away from our normal routines. However, making a change to our daily life could be exactly what we need to break our stress cycle (as explained on page 20) and move forward. Trying something new — whether it's taking a new route to work, starting a new hobby or visiting somewhere different at the weekend — will boost your mood and give you a fresh perspective on life. Often, being somewhere different is enough to free you from your typical day-to-day thoughts and associations. Alternatively, learning a new skill can be very absorbing, and it can also boost your self-confidence as you make progress and see your talents develop.

GET OUTSIDE

A surefire way of reducing your stress levels is to spend time outside enjoying the great outdoors. Simply going for a walk is an instant mood-booster: you'll be out in the fresh air, in touch with the elements and appreciating nature. Most of us can fit a walk into our day, but perhaps you can combine the benefits of being outdoors with a workout by going for a quick jog or bike ride, or even trying your hand at gardening. Studies show that being outside reduces your blood pressure and the level of stress hormones in your body. The benefits of spending time in woods or by the seaside are particularly well documented, but even sitting outdoors and listening to the sound of birdsong or the wind in the trees is incredibly effective and, best of all, it's free!

EMBRACE A ROUTINE

Having a structure to your day or week can be an excellent step towards handling the effects of stress. You may not feel like going to your weekly football session or visiting relatives at the weekend, but stick to your routines if you can, as regular contact with others is essential. If you don't have much of a routine at the moment, start one gradually. Step one could be getting out of bed and getting showered and dressed at the same time each day. Next, make sure you have three regular meal times and stick to them where possible. A regular bedtime routine (see page 45) will improve your sleep. Then add in some regular exercise – even a short walk will pay dividends. When you start to factor in commitments to others, volunteering or regular visits, you are making real progress and will feel valued and more positive too.

OBSERVE YOUR THOUGHTS

//

When we're stressed we are often plagued by negative or anxious thoughts and learning to disengage from these is a useful tool in handling anxiety. When stress strikes, take a step back from your thoughts and remind yourself that they are your mind's natural response to what's happening around you, but that they don't define who you are. (Think of how a bruise doesn't define you as a person; it's just a symptom of something that's happened to you.) Your feelings and thoughts are a little like the weather, so try to relax and remind yourself that stormy times will come and go, but don't get too caught up in them. It can help to meditate on this: sit calmly when you're stressed, focus on your breathing and watch your thoughts slip by as though you're a neutral observer. Breathe through them and remember that this too will pass.

QUICK MOOD-BOOSTERS

If you're struggling to put a positive spin on your day, try a quick fix to boost your mood and de-stress.

- **Compliment someone** – it will boost their mood and yours too.
- **Be grateful** – write down one thing a day that you're grateful for and read through your list regularly.
- **Chat to a friend** – a good chat works wonders, but don't dwell on things. Set a timer, have a rant, try to find a solution together and then talk about something else.
- **Carry out a random act of kindness** – a great option if volunteering seems daunting.

TURN DOWN THE VOLUME

Life in the twenty-first century comes with a soundtrack of background noise and it can be very difficult for us to find a quiet moment during the chaos. The onslaught of noise that surrounds us means that our brains are constantly on alert, albeit on a subconscious level, and we never have time to sit quietly and process what's been happening throughout the day. Turning down the noise can have a hugely beneficial effect on our well-being. Factor in at least ten minutes of quiet time every day with no television or music in the background and all your devices turned off. Use this time to meditate or practise mindfulness; write in your journal or do something creative (that doesn't involve any tech). Bringing some quiet time into your day will reduce your stress levels and improve your quality of sleep too.

PLAN AHEAD FOR STRESS

If you have a stressful event on the horizon, planning ahead can help you to cope when the day arrives. Perhaps you have to make a presentation at work and you're anxious about it. First, remind yourself that it's natural to feel stressed on the day and that eliminating stress completely is not part of your plan because that just isn't realistic. Do all you can to prepare for the event: run through the presentation at home and have some notes of keywords ready in case you lose your thread. Next, work out how to deal with stress on the day – whether it's focusing on your breathing or phoning a trusted friend for a quick morale boost. If a mantra works for you, prepare that too. Work through your plan when the time comes and congratulate yourself for facing your fears. Afterwards, make a note in your journal of how things went and whether there's anything you could improve on for next time.

BE SELECTIVE

The way we refer to tricky situations can have an impact on our stress levels. If you hit a stumbling block in your day, you'll feel better if you refer to it as a "challenge" rather than a "problem", for example. Try to train yourself to use positive language whenever you can and you'll develop a more optimistic attitude to whatever the day brings. Another way of reframing situations is to be selective about what you focus on. If your day was mostly good but you had one tricky conversation with a colleague, try not to dwell on the blip; recall and talk about the good parts of your day instead. (Think of your life as a walk through a beautiful forest: occasionally there will be tricky sections to navigate, and tree roots you have to climb over, but think of all the beauty that makes those obstacles worthwhile – and make that your focus!)

CHAPTER FOUR

THE ANTI-STRESS DIET

Our diet can play an important role in helping us tackle difficult emotions. As stress is a physical reaction that uses up our body's energy and resources, it's important that we consume sufficient nutrients to cope with these extra demands during stressful times. But there's more to beating stress than simply eating a balanced diet, even though it's a great start.

When we become stressed, our levels of adrenaline and cortisol rise, but some foods have the ability to lower the levels of these hormones in our bloodstream and counteract their effects. This chapter shows you how to include these stress-busting superfoods in your diet to promote a feeling of well-being and calm.

Stress itself can affect our diet and appetite. When we feel stressed we might feel tempted to reach for sugar-laden snacks for a quick burst of fight-or-flight energy. However these unhealthy foods can, in the short-term, send our blood-sugar levels into a spin. This can have a negative effect on our mood and, ultimately, affect our weight and overall health. And it's not just what we eat, but how we eat it that matters too, so there are tips in this chapter to help you put a healthy eating plan in place. By making a few simple changes to your diet, you can ensure you're in the best shape to tackle stress when it strikes and keep your stress levels under control.

TO KEEP THE BODY IN
GOOD HEALTH IS A DUTY...
OTHERWISE WE SHALL NOT
BE ABLE TO KEEP OUR MIND
STRONG AND CLEAR.

BUDDHA

A BALANCED DIET

Some foods are good for our stress levels and others are not, but before you start fine-tuning your diet to beat stress, make sure you're eating a good balance of foods regularly throughout the day. You should be eating the right amount of energy-giving foods for your age, height and sex. (Check online to see examples of the rough quantities you should be eating.) Make sure you're also consuming a good variety from across the different food groups, including fibre, protein, unsaturated fats and plenty of fruit and vegetables (for vitamins and minerals). Stress can affect our digestive system in different ways – for instance, chronic stress can lead to gastrointestinal issues like indigestion or constipation – but eating as healthy a diet as possible will help to counteract its effects. A balanced diet will also put you in great shape to fight off stress-induced colds and infections.

CUT OUT REFINED SUGAR

When we're stressed our natural urge can be to reach for something sweet, such as cookies, to fuel our fight-or-flight reflex, but this is actually the worst thing we can do for our stress levels. These "quick fix" products tend to contain large amounts of refined sugar, which cause our blood-sugar levels to spike and then dip. Keep cake and biscuits for an occasional treat when you're feeling in a more positive frame of mind, and opt for fruits and nuts, or a small piece of dark chocolate instead. (See page 117 for more ideas of healthy stress-busting snacks.) Dramatic changes in our blood-sugar level can actually increase the secretion of the stress hormone cortisol, so cutting out processed sugar is a great general de-stressor. Also bear in mind that most cold drinks other than water contain high levels of sugar, so opt for mineral water or herbal teas rather than juice or soft drinks.

CHOOSE THE RIGHT CARBS

Choosing whole, unprocessed carbs – bread, cereals and pasta made from wholegrains, or brown rice – will keep your blood sugar level steady and increase production of serotonin, a hormone that will make you feel calmer and more relaxed. Unprocessed carbs are also digested more slowly than their refined cousins, so they'll leave you feeling fuller for longer. When you realize that they're much better for you too, as they're higher in fibre and they don't get stored as body fat around the waistline, choosing "slow carbs" really makes sense. A surefire way to do this is to avoid wheat altogether and go for other wholegrains and rice, but if that's a step too far, be sure to swap wholegrain pasta, bread and rice into your existing diet, replacing the versions you might normally eat, to see an improvement in your physical and emotional health.

AVOID ALCOHOL

Many people believe that alcohol makes them feel more relaxed, but although you can initially feel less inhibited after a drink, alcohol has depressant qualities and can cause feelings of anxiety as its effects wear off. It can make you prone to mood swings, affects your hormones and, worse still, stress-sufferers can start to depend on alcohol, feeling unable to face difficult situations without having a drink first. Cut back on the booze and, when you do treat yourself to a (small!) glass, pick a wine such as Chianti, Merlot or Cabernet Sauvignon as the grape skins used to make these products contain the sleep hormone melatonin, so they won't be as disruptive to your sleep.

ACE YOUR VITAMIN LEVELS

Vitamins are an essential part of our diet – even more so when we're feeling stressed as the production of stress hormones can deplete our levels of vitamin C. Stress also has a negative impact on the immune system, either making us prone to colds and other infections or over-stimulating it and leaving us struggling with autoimmune disorders, so keep your immune system in peak condition by including vitamins A, C and E in your diet. These are all antioxidants, which boost immunity and reduce inflammation. Vitamin A is found in fish liver oil and egg yolks in the form of retinol (but should be eaten alongside yellow and orange fruits and vegetables, which are beneficial for their beta-carotene content). Include plenty of vitamin C by eating berries and citrus fruit, broccoli and tomatoes. For vitamin E, include nuts, seeds, avocados and olive oil in your diet.

BOOST YOUR VITAMIN B

Vitamin B is another essential nutrient for beating stress. B vitamins control production of tryptophan, which in turn is used by the body to produce serotonin, the so-called "happy hormone". Low levels of tryptophan and serotonin can cause low mood and depression, so be sure to include vitamin B in the form of spinach, broccoli, asparagus, fortified cereal, shellfish or liver in your diet. Vitamin B12, in particular, is only found in animal-based products, so if you are vegan, it is worth considering taking a B-vitamin supplement to boost your intake. Nuts and seeds all contain tryptophan so include these in your diet where possible. In order to absorb tryptophan it's also important to eat plenty of protein – see page 118.

SLOW IT DOWN

When we're under stress we may end up rushing our food or missing meals altogether. Skipped meals mean that we're not getting the steady levels of energy and nutrients we need to fuel us through the day and keep our hormones in balance. And even if we do find the time to eat, sit-down meals can be chaotic and hurried, with us not chewing our food properly or appreciating the flavours. Make more of your mealtimes – sit down, eat slowly and mindfully and really savour the taste of your food rather than resorting to snacks crammed with sugar, salt and fat (see page 102). Even if you only have time for a quick break at work, eat your lunch away from your desk and don't multitask while eating. Try to prepare some healthy snacks ahead too, so you don't end up grabbing a chocolate bar or crisps on the way home. For further guidance on eating more mindfully, see page 126.

MAKE ROOM FOR MINERALS

It's crucial that we eat foods containing enough calcium, magnesium and iron, as all these minerals contribute to a healthy nervous system and help us to maintain a stable mood. Calcium deficiency can trigger anxiety symptoms, so include leafy greens, sesame seeds, kelp and dairy products in your diet. We need magnesium too, to help us absorb calcium, and you can find it in leafy green vegetables, nuts, seeds, wholegrains and seafood. Insufficient levels of iron can cause low mood and anxiety so opt for dark-green vegetables, meat, fish, beans, pulses, nuts and wholegrains. And don't forget zinc – found in broccoli, mushrooms, eggs, seafood, nuts and seeds – because zinc deficiency has been linked to depression.

CHEW SOME CASHEWS!

Cashews contain a host of mood-boosting and stress-busting chemicals in one handy package, so try to have a handful of these every day. First and foremost they're a great source of tryptophan. If we don't eat enough of this amino acid our brain is unable to regulate our mood properly and we can feel anxious, stressed and depressed. (Other good sources of tryptophan include almonds, pumpkin seeds, bananas and sweet potatoes.) Cashews also include high levels of magnesium, which maintains the nervous system and blood sugar levels, along with vitamin B6, which helps our body absorb serotonin, and the mono-unsaturated fats we need to ward off mood dips. If you don't fancy a handful of these nuts as a snack alone, you can get creative and include them in stir-fries or make your own no-bake cashew energy bars – you'll find simple recipes online.

NOURISH YOUR BODY

NURTURE YOUR MIND

ADD ADAPTOGENS

//

Adaptogens are plant products that help us to control stress by regulating our release of cortisol during stressful situations and resetting our fight-or-flight stress response. Many herbs and spices are adaptogens and some are already recognized for their nutritional qualities, including turmeric, liquorice root and maca powder. (Turmeric is particularly easy to find and add to your diet as you can simply sprinkle it on stir-fries or stews.) Goji berries are also adaptogens. Less well-known substances to hunt down are ashwagandha, which also has the added benefit of being a good source of iron, and holy basil, a member of the mint family which has been used in Ayurvedic medicine for centuries. Adaptogens are becoming more well known and you can even find cafes that include these ingredients in smoothies.

STAY HYDRATED

If we don't drink enough water, our bodies can respond to the physical strain of dehydration by producing more stress hormones – and if we're already in a state of anxiety, this can obviously make things worse. Studies show that drinking just half a litre less than we should each day is enough to trigger this reaction. Dehydration can also worsen the symptoms of stress, such as headaches and fatigue, so staying hydrated throughout the day is crucial. The recommended water intake for women is 1.6 litres per day, and for men, 2 litres. Try to carry a bottle of water with you and don't forget that hot drinks and water also add to your daily total. However, take care not to drink too much water as overhydration can lead to low sodium levels in your blood, which can be just as dangerous as dehydration.

AVOID ADDED SALT

The symptoms of stress can cause an imbalance in the body's salt levels and so it's common to crave salty foods when we're feeling anxious. Unfortunately most salty foods are high in the wrong kinds of fats and can cause weight gain and high blood pressure. We can easily end up overcompensating too, as many of us have too much salt in our diets already thanks to "hidden" salt in processed foods and ready meals. Try to be salt-aware and avoid it as an ingredient, snacking instead on raw vegetables and fruit and preparing meals from scratch. You can use other herbs and spices to bring flavour to your meals – a pinch of mixed herbs, oregano or thyme is a much healthier option than reaching for the salt cellar.

TOP DE-STRESS SNACKS

More than just healthy alternatives to your usual snacks, these options will actually help to reduce your stress levels:

- **Pistachios** – lower your blood pressure and heart rate and the process of shelling them by hand can be relaxing too
- **Seeds** – a handy source of magnesium, which regulates mood
- **Dark chocolate** – a square or two lowers your cortisol levels and blood pressure
- **Probiotic yogurt** – calms brain activity and improves gut health
- **Cashews** – for all your de-stress minerals plus tryptophan in one handy snacking package
- **Blueberries** – a superfood packed with antioxidants, blueberries are a great boost to the immune system, essential during stressful times
- **Hummus** – made from chickpeas, which are packed with folates – B vitamins that can help lower stress levels and regulate your mood.

PACK IN SOME PROTEIN

Protein contains the building blocks our body needs to make the hormones and neurotransmitters that keep our mood stable. In times of stress, for example, we use up more tryptophan – that useful substance that stabilizes our mood – so eating plenty of lean protein is essential. Protein foods also have the added bonus of making us feel full for longer and helping us to maintain stable sugar levels. Good sources of protein include lentils, chickpeas, lamb, chicken, fish, soya beans, eggs and cottage cheese. Poached eggs are a particularly good choice, rather than fried or boiled, as the protein in them is not damaged by the cooking process. So a breakfast of poached eggs on wholemeal toast would be a great way to start the day and should stabilize your blood sugar levels and get you through the morning.

EAT THE RIGHT FATS

Essential fatty acids (EFAs) play a vital part in helping the brain function properly. Omega-3, in particular, boosts our neurotransmitters and hormone levels. As well as tackling the effects of stress, this means it helps us to sleep better and avoid blood sugar spikes. Omega-3 is found in fish oil, so try to include sardines, mackerel, salmon or cod in your diet. As well as picking fish for your evening meal, you can get creative and include more fish in your diet by using leftovers in salads or making open sandwiches with fish and salad on wholemeal bread. Or – if you're feeling really brave – why not have kippers for breakfast! Vegans and vegetarians can include chia seeds, Brussels sprouts, walnuts and flax seeds in their diet for a boost of Omega-3.

CUT DOWN ON CAFFEINE

Caffeine is a stimulant and too much of it can trigger the symptoms of anxiety, including an increased heart rate and irritability. Large quantities cause the exhaustion phase of stress which can make us reach for another drink or sugary snack. If you drink a lot of coffee or tea (which contains almost as much caffeine), don't aim to cut it out immediately as caffeine withdrawal can cause headaches, nausea and can destabilize your mood. Instead, cut down gradually over a few days. Ultimately, you should aim for no more than three mugs of tea or coffee a day – about 300 mg of caffeine – but bear in mind that large take-away coffees can include as much as 400 mg in one mug. Herbal teas are a great alternative: rooibos is naturally caffeine-free or try oolong tea, which slows down the firing of neurons in your brain, to help you feel less anxious. Don't forget that caffeine also crops up in colas, chocolate, some painkillers, and exercise supplements, so factor these in too.

CHEER UP MEALTIMES

If eating has become a chore, it's time to mix things up in the kitchen. Is there a dish that you've always wanted to prepare? If so, why not invest in the ingredients and give it a go? Search online for some recipe inspiration or you could even order up a recipe box for a treat. (These boxes are delivered to your door and include everything you need to make two or three tasty meals.) You could organize a cooking evening with some friends, making batches of food together for the week, or you could each provide the ingredients to teach one another your favourite dish. If you don't fancy hosting a cooking fest, you could invite everyone to bring along a course that they've prepared at home. With good food and great company, you'll get two de-stressors in one go!

THE BEST BREAKFASTS

Even if you're in a rush, skipping breakfast isn't a wise option – it will leave you feeling hungry and reaching for the wrong foods later in the day. Eating a balanced breakfast will give you energy to get through the morning and it's a great opportunity to include a few stress-busting foods to help you start the day on an even keel. Great breakfast options include:

- Poached eggs on a piece of wholegrain toast with a little tomato purée
- Scrambled egg with salmon and spinach
- Probiotic yogurt, sprinkled with a handful of berries and a teaspoon of honey
- Porridge with a dash of ginger and sprinkled with almonds
- Flour-free banana and egg "pancakes" with cottage cheese, honey or berries on top
- Smoked kippers and grilled tomatoes

Try to avoid caffeine for your breakfast drink and go for water or a small glass of fruit juice.

LOOK AFTER YOUR GUT

The gut contains a community of beneficial bacteria that don't just influence our digestive system, but our immune system and our mood too. You may have heard it referred to as our "second brain". This is because the gut is formed of the same tissue as your brain and contains 90 per cent of the body's serotonin (the neurotransmitter that helps with mood control), so it's important to take care of it. The bacteria in your intestines flourish on food they can ferment, such as onions, garlic, cauliflower and root vegetables, so include these in your diet regularly. Eating fermented foods, such as kefir, miso, sauerkraut and pickles, is good too. Studies show that looking after your gut health not only boosts your digestive system, but has a direct effect on your brain chemistry, reducing levels of stress hormones and anxiety – a great reason to reach for the pickles!

MINDFUL
MEALS

If you've taken the trouble to prepare a meal, why not eat it as mindfully as possible? Rather than rushing your food while multitasking, switch off any distractions and sit somewhere peaceful to eat. Before you start your meal, take a moment to tune in to your hunger. Then appreciate the details of your meal – the colour and aroma of the food on your plate. As you take a mouthful, close your eyes and chew slowly while you focus on the flavour and texture. At first, when you swallow, mentally trace the path of your food down to your stomach. Does your stomach feel fuller after the first few bites? Savour your meal and think about the way your body feels after you've eaten, appreciating the feeling of fullness and relaxation.

CHAPTER FIVE

GETTING PROFESSIONAL HELP

Tackling stress can be a tough challenge, and there are times when we need a little extra help and support to take it on. If you have tried the other tips in this book – de-stressing your schedule; setting a routine; maintaining contact with others; eating a balanced diet; and learning relaxation techniques – but still feel that stress is getting the better of you, there's a chance that you could benefit from getting professional help.

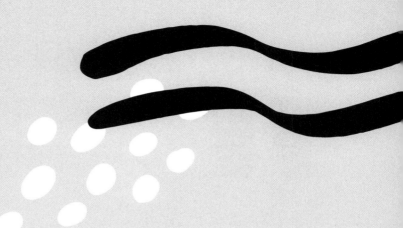

The tips in this chapter describe some of the different treatments and therapies that you can try in order to reduce your stress levels. You'll also learn to recognize the signs of some common anxiety conditions, all of which can be treated with guidance from your doctor.

Your doctor should be your first port of call if your stress is getting out of control. You'll know this is happening if it is dominating your life and you find yourself worrying about worrying, if it's affecting your health and your behaviour, or if you're dependent on unhealthy coping mechanisms, such as drinking, to alleviate the symptoms. Remember that stress is a common problem and you shouldn't feel self-conscious about talking about it. In fact, it's estimated that around 30 per cent of doctors' appointments are with patients who need to discuss stress or anxiety.

This chapter includes tips based on everything from ancient wisdom to the most recent arts-based therapies, so – however stress is affecting you – there are plenty of different avenues you can explore to help you move forward.

HEALING TAKES TIME,
AND ASKING FOR HELP IS
A COURAGEOUS STEP.

MARISKA HARGITAY

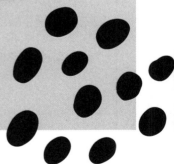

TALK TO YOUR DOCTOR

If stress has become a part of your everyday life or is impacting on your health, booking an appointment with your doctor is the best place to start. Speaking to someone outside of your family or close friends about your worries may seem daunting, but you will feel better for it and they will be in the best position to advise you about treatment options. Make a note of your symptoms before you go, along with any questions you might want to ask. You could also take along a friend for moral support if you like. Your doctor should talk you through the possible causes of your stress and may advise you about counselling, medication or alternative therapies. They may recommend a follow-up appointment to check on your progress.

IDENTIFY ANXIETY DISORDERS

If your stress is manifesting in a particular way, you may be diagnosed with an anxiety disorder. OCD, for example, can cause sufferers to repeatedly perform routines or rituals. Social anxiety disorder can leave people with an overwhelming fear of social situations and being seen in public. Many of us experience phobias – some of which can become severe and may lead us to take extreme steps to avoid the thing we fear most. Others suffer from PTSD, which can make it difficult to recover following a traumatic experience. It's estimated that around 15 per cent of adults suffer from one of these conditions, and if you are one of them at the moment, don't suffer in silence. There is so much support available online and your doctor should be able to recommend the best treatment to help you improve your situation.

TACKLE GENERALIZED ANXIETY DISORDER (GAD)

It may be that you're unable to pinpoint an exact cause for your stress. Rather than worrying about one specific topic, you might find yourself feeling a sense of unease the whole time, leaving you unable to relax. This condition is known as Generalized Anxiety Disorder and your first step in tackling things is to talk through treatment options with your doctor. You will be advised to make any changes you can to improve your health, including stopping smoking if relevant. There are self-help courses that can help you to manage your anxiety levels – which may be carried out on an individual basis or in groups – or you could try CBT (see page 138) or other methods to get things back on an even footing. While seeking treatment can feel like a big step at first, it can help many people learn to deal with long-term stress and control their anxiety levels.

RELAX WITH REFLEXOLOGY

Reflexology is ideal for stress as its specific aim is to reduce tension throughout the body, in order to heal and "rebalance" the person being treated. Practitioners apply gentle pressure to various points on a patient's feet (or hands or ears), which are linked to different parts of the body. There are around 15,000 nerve endings in the feet, for example! The treatment is non-invasive and many people find it deeply relaxing – you might even sleep while it's being carried out. The reflexologist should discuss any concerns with you beforehand but won't diagnose you or give medical advice. For safe, DIY reflexology relief, locate your adrenal reflex on your palm an inch below the base of your thumb. Massage both your left and right hand in turn, using circular movements with your opposite thumb, to feel the stress-busting benefits.

TRY AYURVEDA

An ancient philosophy that teaches us how to balance mind and body, Ayurveda takes a holistic approach to treating the individual based on their *dosha* (the three energies that make up a personality – you can find out your *dosha* online). It combines the use of yoga, plant medicines, massage and the application of oils to correct any imbalances, and has plenty of suggestions for tackling stress. An Ayurvedic practitioner will ask you a series of questions to establish your *dosha* and discover any imbalances, and can then suggest dietary and lifestyle changes, along with herbal supplements to treat you. You could try some Ayurvedic principles yourself to reduce stress, such as: developing a morning routine that includes yoga and breathing exercises; meditating; listening to calming music; and balancing stress with grounding, slow activities. You can discover more about Ayurveda online, and even take a test to discover your *dosha* type and what that means for you.

CHOOSE CBT

Cognitive Behavioural Therapy (CBT) has proved to be a very effective treatment for stress. It's a type of psychological therapy that helps you to replace negative thoughts and behaviours with a more positive approach. It teaches you how your thoughts, feelings and behaviour are linked, and how to use this information to change the way you act when feeling stressed. A typical course of treatment involves an hour-long one-to-one session with a therapist every week for three to four months. Check online for information on how to access CBT therapists in your area – in the UK, the Mind website is a useful starting point (www.mind.org.uk). In particular, you may be referred for this type of therapy following a diagnosis of Generalized Anxiety Disorder (see page 134).

TRY TRAUMA RELEASE EXERCISES (TRE)

TRE – also known as tremoring therapy – can help us release the tension that builds up in our muscles during stressful moments, thanks to the fight-or-flight response. Releasing this tension is something that animals do naturally – shaking after a close encounter with a predator, for example – but humans have lost or suppressed this response, and as a result we have no easy way of releasing our stress naturally. Tremoring is particularly useful for people who have experienced a specific traumatic event, but it can help anyone who needs to release built-up stress, and the exercises should leave you feeling relaxed and calm. It is safe, and not painful or uncomfortable. It's important to see a trained therapist at first as there may be side-effects if the practice is not performed correctly.

CONSIDER COUNSELLING

Counselling is another effective talking therapy that can help stress-sufferers to improve their symptoms. It involves discussing your feelings with a trained therapist, who will listen to you without criticism or judgement. Your therapist can help you to understand why you feel the way you do, and can guide you in moving forward, but they won't tell you what to do. Counselling sessions can take place over the phone, by email or online as well as in a traditional one-to-one setting. For the best chance of improvement, you should find a therapist that you're comfortable with. The number of sessions you'll need will depend on your situation, but most people need several sessions before they see an improvement.

HEAL WITH HYPNOSIS

Hypnosis can be used to treat stress in two ways: firstly, it can help us to access a relaxed state (a "trance"), which is a huge benefit to the stress-sufferer whose body may be constantly in a state of fight-or-flight. Secondly, during a guided session by a trained hypnotherapist, the patient can enter a trance and receive positive suggestions to help them relax and deal with their stress more effectively. It's worth knowing that during hypnosis the patient is always aware of what they are doing and always in control. Hypnosis takes a little practice and certainly isn't for everyone, but the potential benefits could make it worth trying.

BENEFIT FROM BEHAVIOURAL ACTIVATION

This talking therapy, which is used in CBT and other behavioural therapies, uses the link between our actions and emotions to improve our feelings and tackle problems such as stress and depression. Stress can affect the way we behave – we can avoid challenges when stressed, for example – but this behaviour only reinforces our feelings of anxiety in the long run. Working with a therapist, it's possible to learn to schedule in positive activities, such as socializing or hobbies, that will lessen feelings of stress. Behavioural activation involves learning to self-monitor stress levels, to schedule and structure the week, to problem solve during tricky moments and to set short-term and long-term goals to improve things moving forward. These are all great stress-busting skills and there are even worksheets online that you can use to try some of these elements out at home.

ASKING FOR HELP IS NOT A SIGN OF WEAKNESS

IT'S A SIGN OF INNER STRENGTH AND WISDOM

TRY
ACUPUNCTURE

Acupuncture is a treatment in which fine needles are inserted into pressure points throughout the body. A lot of research has been carried out into its effectiveness for treating stress and depression, with positive results. The treatment is based on traditional Chinese medicine, which identifies blockages in the body's energy pathway. These blockages are removed when the needles are inserted. A treatment session is tailored to your individual needs. It will begin with the therapist gathering information about your health and doing simple physical checks, such as examining your tongue and taking your pulse, which can reveal much more about your health than just your heart rate. The needles will be left in for up to half an hour; most people find the treatment very relaxing and it may include aromatherapy and soothing music. It's important to visit a licensed and registered therapist, so check online to find one near you.

SORT WORKPLACE STRESS

Work is the most common cause of stress in our lives, whether it's our workload, working conditions or troubles with our colleagues. No one will feel happy in their job every day, but if you've been struggling for a while and work stress impacts on your life as a whole, you should take positive steps to improve your situation. Speak to your manager or Human Resources representative: make a note beforehand of any questions you'd like to ask, such as whether you can have extra training or work flexible hours. If you don't feel supported by your employer, you could also seek advice and support from an association, such as the Citizens Advice in the UK.

TRY A STRESS WORKSHOP

Some workplaces offer stress-management workshops, which involve a combination of de-stressing exercises and tips for identifying and handling workplace stress. The workshops can be hugely beneficial to a company, increasing productivity and morale, and reducing sick leave due to stress. If your workplace doesn't offer this at the moment, talk to your colleagues: if there's a demand for one, your boss may consider arranging a workshop for everyone to attend. Alternatively, you can attend stress-management workshops independently. A typical programme includes learning to identify stress, assessing your current coping strategies, acquiring simple mindfulness skills, learning how to say no, and creating an action plan for handling stress in the future.

TURN TO ART THERAPY

Taking part in a creative or expressive activity is an excellent way of reducing stress and if this appeals to you, you may find arts-based therapy a more appealing approach than a traditional counselling session. Check online for more information and links to help you explore what's available, but broadly speaking you can try dance movement therapy, drama therapy, music therapy or a visual arts-based approach. You don't need to have any prior experience to carry out any of these treatments and they can be particularly beneficial if you find it a challenge to express your feelings verbally. Therapists are trained to respond to the way you express yourself and suggest ways to use the relevant media to help you feel more positive.

RELAX WITH REIKI

//

Reiki is a complementary therapy in which the practitioner channels healing energy into a patient and can remove blockages around their energy centres, known as chakras. The treatment is non-invasive and shouldn't hurt. Patients relax on a treatment table while the practitioner holds their hands over, or rests them gently upon, the patient's chakras – in particular the areas where we tend to hold a lot of stress. Even if you are unsure about the science behind the treatment, there is no denying the calming effects of a session, which often involves an hour of relaxation where the patient's sole focus is on the sensations of their body and the calming surroundings of the treatment room. While the demands of modern-day life often trigger our fight-or-flight mode, Reiki activates our rest-and-repair mode instead and is a perfect antidote to stress.

HERBAL HELP

If you prefer to avoid prescription medication, there are several herbal remedies that can help you manage the symptoms of stress. St John's wort increases serotonin activity in the brain and includes other useful mood-boosting substances too. Valerian root is often used to treat anxiety and aid sleep. Passion flower, which can be taken as drops or tablets, contains a compound that slows down brain activity, helping you to relax. Or you could try taking Rhodiola rosea extract – an adaptogen (see page 114) which has been shown to improve the symptoms of stress. Check with your pharmacist before taking herbal remedies in case they react with any medication or existing medical conditions.

LET LOOSE WITH WITH LAUGHTER THERAPY

If you're feeling stressed, laughing is probably the last thing that springs to mind, but laughter has a beneficial effect on the body, physically and emotionally. Laughter boosts your intake of oxygen, relaxes your muscles and releases endorphins (improving your mood). It also benefits your immune system and helps you to distance yourself from your worries. You can try laughter therapy in group or individual sessions, which will combine gentle warm-up exercises with anything from role play to learning how to fake laughter to feel the benefits of a good giggle. You can introduce more laughter into your life yourself by watching your favourite sitcom, going to a comedy club or creating a collage of humorous pictures, quotes or greetings cards that put a smile on your face. Practise laughing at home if you can – even if you have to fake it! A fake laugh will still mimic the effects of a real one, so the benefits will be just as powerful.

BREATHE
IN

BREATHE
OUT

FURTHER
HELP

Stress is recognized as a huge problem throughout society, and as a result there is a lot of information, help and support available for stress-sufferers. Check online for charities, counsellors and other therapists that offer information on coping with stress, and helplines that you can call if you feel that stress is taking over your life, or if you simply need advice on what to do to manage your symptoms. The International Stress Management Association is a charity that offers access to support services, and there are numerous other online groups and associations that can help you to improve your situation. Simply search online for stress management advice in your area. Check out relevant forums and blogs too – the online community has a wealth of useful stress-busting experience to offer. Help is available. It's there for you, so don't be afraid to use it.

CONCLUSION

Stress affects all of us, at one point or another, so it's important that we all have our own tactics for dealing with it. Hopefully this book has provided you with plenty of ideas for how to find calm in any situation. And remember, even the smallest step forward is still a step in the right direction! Be proud of yourself for even just making the decision to improve your lifestyle.

If you've given everything a try and your worries are still proving too much for you to deal with, it could be time to seek professional help. Visit a medical professional and see what they suggest for you. Be honest with them and give as much detail as possible, as this will help them find the right solution for you. Complementary therapies can help to reduce your stresses and strains, but sometimes professional help is what's needed.

So, take care of yourself – and enjoy your journey toward a happier, calmer you!

If you're interested in finding out more about our books, find us on Facebook at **Summersdale Publishers**, on Twitter at **@Summersdale** and on Instagram at **@summersdalebooks**.

www.summersdale.com